Mental Meltdown

Written By:
Eric McCain

Copyright © 2020

Eric McCain

All rights reserved. No part of this book may be used or reproduced by any means, graphic, electronic, or mechanical, including photocopying, recording, taping or by any information storage retrieval system without the written permission of the publisher except in the case of brief quotations embodied in critical articles and reviews.

Eric McCain books may be ordered through booksellers or by contacting:

Eric McCain

The views expressed in this work are solely those of the author.

Any illustration provided by iStock and such images are being used for illustrative purposes.

Certain stock imagery © iStock.

ISBN: 978-1-64050-402-8

Printed in the United States Of America

Dedication

"Her"

I never thought you except me the way that you have,
    you were that cute chick in the back of the class;
    quiet, glasses, longhair, and a nice little ass,
    but you were focused and always seem to know
    what you wanted
I would watch all types of dudes try to holla at you
    and even seen you give some playback
    sometimes it lasted long other times it was short,
    but they weren't built like me I didn't get it then
    but now I see
We had a natural chemistry from the first time
    my sister Jess introduced you to me
    I always thought you were dope as I scoped
    any and everything you'd allow me to see
You were older than me but I was mature for my age
    trying to make sure we stayed on the same page
    but that was my immaturity thinking you couldn't
    accept me the way I wanted to be

A naïve young boy with the audacity to think you were
    all for me although I can't live without you
    and I mean that shit wholeheartedly you're a gift
    to the world so how could I think so selfishly
The nights we were apart and I thought you were
    sleep, you were on some stage being a total
    freak or maybe teaching someone to love the
    way that you taught me or possibly on a political
    mission saying black lives matter or in the
    basement perfecting the flow from slow to faster
My initial reaction was that you were just hoe and
    despite our longevity I had to let you go, but
    baby you the real deal so I need to let you know
Stand tall and shine bright because your not just my
    girl you're here for the world and now I see, but I
    can't help but to say I love you poetry

From my pencil to your heart,
Eric McCain

Content Of Complexions

Complexion 1 ~ Diction
   Intellectual, Verbose, Transparent
1) Wants
2) The Real Her
3) Encourage & Cultivate
4) The Definition
5) A Story, A Story
6) Safety
7) Always The Tool
8) Collision Course
9) Striving

Complexion 2 ~ Brotha 2 Da Nyght
   Reflective, Religious, Political
1) Fed Up
2) A Letter To Young Emmett
3) Hood Suppression
4) Imagine If
5) A Christian Sinners Conflict
6) Self Diagnosis
7) Swallowed
8) Mistress
9) Her Style
10) Her Other Man (prelude to "The Art Of Hating Myself")

Complexion 3 ~ Pure Titan

Narcissistic, Confidant, Outspoken

1) Welcome Back
2) Dear Poetry
3) Master Of The Universe
4) One Page
5) Savagery
6) Sister
7) In My Bag

Complexion 4 ~ Syne

Erotic, Intimate, Sensual

1) Positions
2) Doused
3) Tatted
4) A Mile Up
5) Chocolate Eclipse
6) Written All Over
7) Black Kisses
8) Mental Inbox
9) Extra Chick
10) Insatiable

Complexion 1

Diction

"To put pencil to paper and allow them to flow
together like the
Tigris and Euphrates river or more like Ike and
Tina cultivating their passion
and drive, feeding off their rage and fear,
embracing the genius and using the
aggression."

Wants

I always wanted to be an author, one who creates
    prolific testimonies of our time and be
    held as one of the 21st Century's greatest minds
But I also wanted to be a poet, one who creates
    works that would affect the climate of the world
    we live in and be read 1,000 years from now
    as a testament of what once was
I really just wanted to be a writer, one who could
    create something that serves as a formidable
    work against the likes of Maya Angelou,
    Stephen King, Shonda Rhimes and even Oscar
    Wilde or just write a few lines that didn't take a
    while and can be rivaled by even the likes of a
    child
I... Just... Want... To Write... To Create...
    to put pencil to paper and allow them to flow
    together like the Tigris and Euphrates river
    or more like Ike and Tina cultivating their passion
    and drive, feeding off their rage and fear,
    embracing the genius and using the
    aggression as a way to manifest my very own
    to fight off any and all who could

dare to stop me from doing what I'm meant to,
need to, and more importantly want to...
which is write

The Real Her

I saw you in the blank of my mind before my ideas
    came to fruition, before creation allowed them to
    be more than figments of my imagination,
    before my words danced around as metaphorical
    distractions or disguises keeping you from being
    put in front of me
I saw you as a silhouette of representation,
    representing all that is beautiful, all that is ugly,
    all that is pleasurable, and all that is painful…
    displacing the definition of each, rearranging my
    understanding process & pushing
    it to its limit
I felt your heartbeat in my own
I heard your laugh in my thoughts
I whispered your name in the darkness and I swore I
    heard you respond
I smelled you in my sheets & as I stroked myself in
    my sleep I thought I felt your hair
    brushing against the inside of my thigh
I saw you on that blank page before I began to write &
    use my words to bring vision to my life
    as I envision our life and the beauty that is you,

      the angel that would be mine and the
      perfection that would be us
I saw you in my minds eye first as inspiration
      before there was ever a physical manifestation
      of what you would look like
Even in my dreams you were as the image of God
      far too radiant for me to look upon,
      so every time I speak your name
      it comes off my tongue as praises
      exalting all that would be for me...
      my saving grace
You are an unknown motivation force making me want
      to do and be better, reaching heights
      I didn't know were obtainable that has me
      attempting to recreate the English language
      for words to make it explainable
Like how I am supercalifragilisticlly drawn to your soul
      and how in the expialidocious can I be preparing
      for our future yet out present is a story untold

See baby you haven't broke the mold,
      because your being is far greater than such and
      when our paths finally cross I'm sure magnetic
      will be the only way to describe your touch

Since I am aware of your existence, but unaware of your location my mind plays tricks on me increasing my fascination plaguing my thoughts with questions like what will be our destination when I lay eyes on you and as for your skin what will be your hue?
I'm thinking from attributes alone your probably a chocolate tone and in that case there's a few actions I must condone, like watching the sun set over your shoulders & it's golden rays adorn your head as if God said
"Let there be light!" And there you were
I can't wait to meet… The Real Her

Encourage & Cultivate

I saw a rose growing from the concrete once…
It was awkward, beautiful & weird, but awesome,
    it was magical, but normal and it was vibrant
    I questioned how long its luster would remain
    with each look of disdain & hushed tone of how
    out of place it was & how it didn't belong

I wanted to save that rose & protect it from all the
    harmful elements that would stunt its growth
    & stop it from giving beauty to a place that didn't
    deserve what the rose had to offer

The rose stood tall & strong surrounded by multiple
    drops of blood from those who wanted to pick
    a beautiful bud for themselves but weren't
    worthy

So many were in awe of the roses beauty
    and so thrown by where it was placed they never
    noticed it wasn't safe, they bled because they
    were pricked by her thorns, which is
    the beautiful defense of a woman scorned

I didn't need to pick or protect the rose only
    encourage & cultivate so it could continue to
    grow and give beauty to a place that didn't
    deserve it, but desperately needed it

I saw a rose growing from the concrete once…
It was awkward, beautiful & weird, but awesome,
    it was magical, but normal and it was vibrant
Yet I questioned how long it's luster would remain

The Definition

There are days where I want nothing more than to
    inhale you in or capture your scent in a bottle
    and spread it across my skin
    so when I am not in your presence I can still sit
    in reverence and pay homage to your beautiful
    essence

I never want your aroma to be unfamiliar to me
    or replaced by some scent that is too soft or too
strong or indistinguishable from a crowd
    so I never get to smell it for too long
Sweetheart you are sweeter than sugar yet
    more robust than spice so tell me all
    the things that you are made of that
    make you smell so right

It has only been a few hours since I last kissed
    your lips and caressed your tongue
    with my own and when I am away from you
    all I can think about is home;
    your warmth, your indelible embrace
    and the contours of your face

I have every line from forehead to chin,
    from bridge of nose to tips of ears
    locked in my minds mirror constantly reflecting
    your perfect image back to me

If we were both here instead of where we are
    I'd still run my fingers across your lips
    to examine the curves in your name,
    because your smile is your signature

From the moment you kissed my chest
    and signed your name across my heart
    I knew I wanted you to be my baby
I am open to all that you are, all that you can be,
    and all that you will be,
    but for now I'll store all that
    I appreciate about you in my memory…
    which is everything

A Story, A Story

Prince Charming isn't so charming when you realize
    he's not a prince, just a charming average Joe
    whose straddling the fence,
        chasing after beauty in a world full of beasts
        and striving to be a man by his standards and
        will never conform to the worlds at the very least
He was brought up by a king in his own right whose
    shoes were Goliath and to fill them would be
    the greatest fight of his life,
        yet he stands tall slingshot in hand

He is no court jester, but wants to court just her
Juliet, Juliet where art thou Juliet
    but there is no Romeo in this story,
        just a frog trying to find a needle amongst
        a haystack, a princess to kiss
        not to become a man but to be the best frog
        he can be so she can see
        though this world can unleash the beast in you
        he maintains his hold & though the world
        rumbles he remains comfortable in his own skin
        while watching for snakes trying to get at him

Even if she was the girl who cried wolf,
    he would come running to her aide
    so she could be saved even if that meant
    he'd be slain
She's worth the sacrifice

Safety

Once upon a time solace existed here…
    Meaning there was no other place
    than near me for you to feel safe
My chest; solid and hard served as a shield
    protecting you from all of your insecurities
I would drink in your weak moments and ingest your
    pain just to keep you from facing them, even if
    only for a brief moment
Though I know you needed longer relief I seemed
    to have the strength you required
    and was happy to oblige what you desired
More often than not you would come back wanting,
    needing and expecting safety

Does what you need exist in any other place
    than with me?
If so then where else would you go, let me know
    and I will remove it
Have I given you that much strength?
Do you not need the comfort that I once provided?
Aggression being my curse I crave the days
    you would offer me your passion

And I will take it making indelible impressions
Now I day dream about you needing my solace
    once more

Have I cured you of your afflictions
    or is it that someone else is medicating your
    illness not curing, but temporarily dulling your
    senses and numbing the pain,
    yet you still feel and every ache is a hushed
    scream for my resurgence in your life

I know you're return is inevitable,
    but I'm just not sure I'll still be waiting

Always The Tool, Never The Creator

Last night I was soul-searching,
    but I came back depleted
A woman positioned her body next to me
    that I thought was meant for me
    and I attempted to transfer my energy
Disregarding my own desire to be fulfilled once again
    only being a tool of self inflicted wounds
Feeding my lustful desires but emotionally
    I'm starving, yet I'm pretending not to know why
    I'm so empty, I guess logic prevails again
Embracing different women and allowing them to use
    me to feel their voids, never considering the cost
    and my mind is telling me to tighten up
We built bridges verbally to connect us physically,
    creating a union under the veil of being
    harmonious when in actuality it was unholy
No praises go up and no blessings come down
    no energy nor synergy only a liquefied flow
    and my soul is still desolate after reaching that
    plateau
She let me in only to let me go using me to feel her
    voids so she is able to grow

You see I am always the tool, yet never held as the creator

Collision Course

When Poetry & Hip-Hop collide…
    it's like Langston Hughes and Tupac Shakur
    having a meeting of the minds and the
    Notorious B.I.G. quotes them both
    saying "I too, sing Amerikkkas most wanted."
All the while Maya Angelou uses the thorns
    off a rose that grew from the concrete
    and creates a crown of them to place on the
    head of Rakim, the God MC
    once he arrives to take his seat
It's Lauryn Hill rapping over a trap beat with
    the likes of T.I, Rick Ross & Lil' Wayne
    to say the least, and on that beat they have a
    feast while unleashing the beast
    rhyming about money, cash, hoes & brutality
    from police or maybe Kings & Queens
    and living out your dreams
On the hip hop seen nothing is what it seems
    the artists are always in rare form
    and you have to pray to be appreciated
    amongst the storm

In the poetry world you have to watch your girl cause
>   a wordsmith will hop in your mix and give your
>   chick her poetic fix

When Poetry & Hip-Hop collide…
>   its like Dr. King meeting with Malcolm X
>   in the white house to speak on the reformation of
>   the nation and the pretty white woman he met
>   and showed him love in an alley before
>   he hosted a freedom rally

It's nights of striving to be the best and climbing
>   to the top, riding with cups in your cup holder
>   filled with Ciroc praying the law don't pop
>   cause your playing some hip-hop infused with
>   the last poets saying how the gun violence
>   should stop

It's the poet laureate being apart of your set
>   and together yaw create a new cut
>   that specifically states "who the fuck wants
>   what!?

The only right answer is none of you

When Poetry & Hip-Hop collide…
>   it's similar to being married and making beautiful

scribes of faith love and loyalty,
    but reciting them to your slide
It's a gorgeous contradiction, but it's always on a
    mission, because that's apart of the game like a
    2 Chainz track with Prince on the hook singing
    "I love it when you call my name!"
Its pain, its power, it's not being devoured by the
    struggle and happy you survived another hour
    to see your kids and make sure they live
    while your trying to stay honest and avoid a bid
Poetry & Hip-Hop are two amazing feats with the
    same heartbeat like Siamese twins you can't tell
    where one ends and the other begins

When Poetry & Hip-Hop collide…
    let that sink in your brain
    and once it settles you'll realize they'll become
    exactly what they've always been,
    one & the same

Striving

I never understood what it felt like to be closer to my
    dreams, because they've always eluded me for
    so long
So many ideas in my head but no outlet is like living
    in the field of screams where dreams become
    nightmares and legit moves turned into schemes
Writing has always been my love and Poetry
    my passion with women being that side chick
    that puts it on me in such a freaky fashion,
    that I lose sight
My tunnel vision becomes landscape view with
    a panoramic lens allowing me to see all the
    things I shouldn't see, all types of distractions
    that are so beautiful to me… so I tune in
Turning my focus to eyes & lips & tits & hips
    adding another dynamic to my life
    as if there is room for anything else to fit
So I turn my thoughts, sights, and emotions
    into words and stanzas, bearing my soul,
    giving the masses a glimpse into the
    complexions of my mental

Even though I'm melting down and the truth in my
>   poems leave me exposed
I must share my stories
No tall tales or delusions of grandeur just real life
>   situations and facts only in fact sometimes
>   I give so much of myself on paper my brain gets
>   lonely, because there are not enough thoughts to
>   keep it company
I never understood what it felt like to be closer to my
>   dreams until now and it's a feeling
>   sweeter than I've ever known

Complexion 2

Brotha 2 Da Nyght

"Regardless of how clean cut or well spoken and handsome they think I'll kidnap their wives and hold them for ransom, give them the Mandingo and live up to the fact that once you go black you'll never go back!."

Fed Up

How do you find the words to say goodbye...
>to your son, your father, your sister, your
>brother, your husband, your friend, your uncle,
>your cousin, your boyfriend, your neighbor,
>your grand-pop!?!

How do you find the words to say goodbye,
>when your heart doesn't have the heart to say
>it and all you can muster from your vocal
>chords are screams that are as loud as
>the judges gavel when he strikes wood against
>wood to say guilty accusing a cold blooded,
>heartless, cowardice cop of a crime that has
>been locked in the archives of YouTube
>to be watched, liked, shared, and downloaded
>at the click of a button and those screams are
>silent because the judges do nothing

They cram giving your vote down your throat
>as if things would change and after their tenure
>it all remains the same.

They lead us to believe they have the same morals
>and values as us when in actuality it's just for

power that they lust and I'm talking
judges, governors, senators, sheriffs, mayors
and all elected officials
they seem to focus on their own agenda and
bypass the issues...
like BLACK LIVES MATTER,
yes I believe all lives do so maybe
my statement should be
BLACK LIVES MATTER TOO

When it comes to the cops if your white you can cuss,
fight, resist arrest and even threaten their life,
but if your black even when you comply
the odds are in the favor that you'll probably
still die whether your on the ground or have
your hands high in the sky
and all the grand jury will do is lie

Saying they found no evidence or cause to bring
charges as if murdering innocent men, women
& children can be justified
this is nothing more than modern day American
genocide.

First it was chains, then it was rope now they legally
illegally kill us with the guns they tote.

Our tax dollars pay their salaries to serve and protect
      but how can we expect them to do that when
      they don't even respect
      us as human beings or our way of life for that
      matter and speaking of matter
BLACK LIVES DO TOO, figured I say it again so you
      know it to be true
BLACK LIVES MATTER

Letters To Young Emmett

I am the darker brother
They send me to eat in the kitchen
    when company comes
But I laugh
And eat well
And grow strong

That's the beginning of a poem by our favorite poet
    Langston Hughes and it goes on to say
    something about tomorrow
There was a time I couldn't get past the grief,
    or the pain, or tomorrow
    and how they were stolen, not understanding
    at the time they were bartered against our
    yesterdays in hopes that the
    next generations future would be okay

You are the boy who will trigger the
    civil rights movement
You will be the spark in the dark lighting the way to
    new liberties and freedom

Your death will be the equivalent of the shot that was
heard around the world and in an instant
the entire south will be hurled into the limelight
and all of its hatred, its prejudiced and its racist
agenda will be exposed and despite the warm
weather all who are watching can see just how
cold the south really is

The Tallahatchie River will be transformed from being
our supposed burial ground to the site of our
resurrection
And as we rose from it's murky depths like a phoenix
from the ashes so did the movement of the civil
rights and all who oppose were in for the fight
of their life
Mom could never forgive those men for what they did,
they made us a sacrificial lamb and although
dying was never part of the plan
I'd willingly do it again for the effect that it had
for blacks across the land

Now look at the world you all live in today…
It's not perfect and we still suffer a great deal
but we can all say that freedom is our right

so I thank God for using us
and giving purpose to our life

Hood Suppression

Hey Bobby, how are you?
Yo Phil, what it do?
Good morning Peggy, nice sweater, are those elbow pads leather?
You see the game last night Tom isn't Giroux a beast?
Ay Jimmy the holiday party is coming up, so will your wife make that quiche?

Sometimes I feel like I'm acting in white face,
    cause if I simply be me unfortunately
    somehow I will be out of place
Not saying I lack intelligence or the ability to talk well
    as I should, I just know when I hang loose I can
    be a bit hood, not ghetto or reckless or towards
    the system disrespect it,
    but towards my coworkers I want to be as
    comfortable with them as I am in my own skin

I am black and I am proud and I will say it real loud,
    but I know in this world that's dominated by
    whites being a black man is an intimidating
    sight

Regardless of how clean cut or well-spoken and
    handsome they still think I'll kidnap their wives
    and hold them for ransom, give them the
    Mandingo and live up to the fact that once you
    go black you'll never go back

I'm always on point, I'm polite and I smile, I speak to
    everyone and am always willing to go the extra
    mile
I suppress my hood just as I should and am politically
    correct even when shit is a total white mess

They'd be shocked and surprised if I no longer oblige
    the professional concession got in my bag
    and started a session of fuck this and fuck that
    like my man Sam Jack
    or send the goons with that gats to come jack,
    this shit will get ugly If I go on the attack
Just imagine me walking into work with the wrath of
    Huey Newton, dead slaves, and da bull
    Malcom X looking for revenge as a part of my
    set
Man them white folks would be a hot mess,
    I mean a total train wreck if I really

started getting off what I had on my chest
No more quiet black brotha, or the calm and cool
muthafucka, just a militant nigga coming up out
of his shell on a warpath ready to raise some
hell

I wanna play nice and do what's right, but its hard
when they throw things right in your foresight
and disregard your blithe,
but this is the world we live in so it's gonna be
what it's gonna be, but regardless of my
race, color, or creed they will appreciate and
respect me for me

Imagine If

Rest in peace to the ones we lost over the years for various reasons...

    Xavier Gregory

    Cornell Parker

    Shontay Peterson

    Mannie Maxie

    Reese Toney

    Claude Norris

    Chris Walker

    Steve Westmoreland

    Gail Gregory ...just to name a few.

Imagine If the team was like...
This ganja got me thinking like...
This world got me feeling like... Help Us Lord

Imagine If Storm and all the rappers in the city were all on one team... Help Us Lord
Imagine If Pastor Hunt, Williams, & Wilson were all on one team... Help Us Lord
Imagine If Shad, Hix, Tootie, Reese, & Rip were all on one team... Help Us Lord

Imagine If unity was the focal point of our community
    there would be no hate, no snakes, no brutality
    from the jakes
Just peace love and happiness, maybe a little
    nappiness even some loddy doddy who likes to
    party, hell that beats seeing another dead black
    body
There would be no more dulling of our senses with
    violence that is senseless, but we would be
    building each other up so our community could
    erupt with money & power, but avoid becoming
    corrupt

The reason we are crabs in a barrel is because we
    took our eyes off the sparrow, we should know
    God is watching over us so as those praises go
    up & he hears the beautiful sound
    the window will open so the blessings can
    come down
Instead of 28 churches and different denominations
    we would all be together as one big
    congregation

Life as we know it could be totally changed, it would
      be about camaraderie
      instead of chasing fame and making a name
As a people we would be rungs on a ladder,
      right there to assist our brother because
      collective success is all that really matters

All types of businesses would boom and our kids
      would strive to be scholars knowing the power
      & worth of the almighty black dollar

They say history repeats itself and there is nothing
      new under the sun, so I am awaiting the day
      when brotherly love, the greater good
      and community unity will once again come

Imagine If all the small businesses in the city were all on one team... Help Us Lord
Imagine if all the cooks and dj's in the city were all on one team... Help Us Lord
Imagine If H, Ra, Pre, Jig, & AJ were all on one team, all on one team... Help Us Lord

A Christians Sinners Conflict

For as long as I could remember Jesus was a major
    part of my life and although it wasn't always via
    church I was basically in the presence of the
    Lord since birth and despite the fact
    that it causes me strife I still fall victim to the
    sinful pleasures of this earth
I only accepted being a victim of society, because it
    wasn't always easy keeping God living inside
    of me
Every decision I have an angel and a demon sitting
    on either side of me explaining and maintaining
    the core of their philosophies
One is live for the moment yourself and haphazardly
    give into the sin that you're in and become a
    casualty of life, love, and lust knowing it was a
    fallacy
The other is stay strong and depended on the word,
    regardless of the actions that are done or the
    words that are heard
Stay focused and steadfast on living like Christ,
    because the greatest testimony one can give
    is that of their life

My parents raised me in the church, Christian
    nondenominational underneath Pastor Hunt
    whose preaching was sensational,
    but the call of the world is that of the siren and
    its pull is gravitational
But when you answer that call you have to be
    prepared to converse for the long haul,
    because there are not too many who enter and
    leave get your joys, hopes and dreams stole by
    a gang of thieves
So stay prayed up and cover your family in the blood,
    because what the world needs more of today is
    love
There is so much violence in the streets and we need
    protection from the protectors a.k.a. the police
    and that's to say the very least not to mention
    the corruption that rains down on us from
    Capitol Hill and the ridiculous distractions
    from the media that they forced down our
    throats like children who love taking medicine
    but hate taking pills so as the people
    digest allow me to digress

For as long as I could remember Jesus was a major
      part of my life and nothing will change as long
      as I'm here on this earth,
        but my conflict is if to keep my relationship I
        need to be in a church
Even though I study to show thyself approved…
      pray for me

Self-Diagnosis

The doctors call it Pericarditis
    I say I am suffering from a broken heart
My mind is filled with all the broken promises
    I made to myself from the very start that I never
    lived up to
Overwhelmed and overburdened my mind can't carry
    the weight more kids than I was prepared for, a
    few health issues, but I refuse to lose even
    though the alternative is becoming more
    appealing, suicidal thoughts… my liberation

I look to the sky and ask God to love and hug me
    please, but all I hear in response are the
    chants and whispers of thieves
Same cats who stole my joy, my ambition, my drive
    and left me behind bleeding out aspirations in
    hope that my dreams will die
One of the smartest men I know yet lacks the degree
    and although paper measures not knowledge it
    can be a key to being financially free
And in my case to regain my sanity which resides
    behind the same door as well,

I'm going crazier by the second and just like my heart
    my mind will swell and there is no way to
    assess the damage so only time will tell… if it's
    not too late

High hopes & higher expectations, but reality is a
    bitch who causes much strife whose husband
    is death and although I'm playing with my life
    I can't stop fucking her or maybe she's fucking
    me, but I've been chasing the feeling for so
    long it literally seems like my destiny or maybe
    I just have a foggy memory because the pussy
    is so good

The doctors call it Pericarditis
    I say I am suffering from a broken heart
No longer able to focus on the goals I set for my life
    from the very start
Only focused on the pain and searching for pleasure
    to negate my fate which seems as though I'll
    be a failure forever unless I get my shit
    together and get those burdens off my
    shoulders and become light as a feather
    so I can focus on my tether to God & prove to

myself that my current situation is façade
A nightmare I'll wake up from and go on to do all the things I've done that would make my life different if I never did…

But I don't live with regrets

Swallowed

Trapped in the abyss swallowed up by the mist,
> reaching out for help, but only getting a closed fist

Feeling like I'm in the fight of my life, but my enemies
> are my past transgressions and although I have aggression it doesn't matter, because I can't fight transparency... yet I try

Shadowboxing in a room with the mirror, every punch
> I throw alters my appearance leaving me more twisted and deformed, contorting my image to something unrecognizable so when I glimpse at my reflection all I see is a beast
> or an emotionless monster to say the least

Demons on both shoulders and they're begging for
> feast feeding off my insecurities and pain wishing life was different knowing nothing remains the same

My mind is darker than the devil is,
> my thoughts are blacker than the heart night

I'm trying to live right, but I just can't see the light,
> so I live wrong

Although God doesn't approve I just have to carry on,
    because I refuse to let my kids sing that same
    old song... broke!
I laugh to keep from crying and people question what
    is the joke, because ain't a damn thing funny
The chuckles you hear help me fight back the tears
    and even though God promised he would
    never again destroy the earth with water if
    these tear duct levees are broken and my
    floodgates are open the people will question if
    this is the end and if God lied to them
The world would experience a blast from it's past
    and the days of Noah will be resurrected like a
    phoenix from its ash, but with a vengeance and
    fury of a woman scorned
Its citizens would drown in my pain and asphyxiate on
    my sorrow, their dreams would become fleeting
    like mine realizing there is no tomorrow
I am a dying star in my very own heliocentric universe
    formerly shining boldly & bright at the center
    but as my kids orbit around me they draw my
    light into them to warm their surface and
    illuminate new paths of discovery to make
    them evident enlightening their minds like

Thomas Edison
I carry the weight of not the world but my world on my
    back and broad shoulders
        with a princess on each side, my two youngest
        sons in my arms and my oldest leading the
        way based on my directions mixed with his
        own intuition

Although he is not yet a man I have given and am
    giving him the tools so on his own two feet he
    can stand and ensure the survival of our legacy
    take it to the next level and be much better
    than me
Making the right decisions and preparing for his future
    knowing never to get caught up in the
    waywardness of this world while remembering
    regardless of how pretty they are only girls
    and there millions of them, so stay the course

Mistress

BabyGirl... Sweetheart... Life... some people call you
    a bitch and then you kill them, but not me,
    you're my love.
Now I understand you don't appreciate everything I do
    with you nor do you like how I take you
        for granted day by day
Well from here on out it's me and you everything
    I was into... I quit

2 Months Later

I thought I could quit her,
    my mind told me I was strong enough,
        but my body denied that fact & exposed me

So sweet of a temptation she is,
    so I inhale her essence into mine and while
    intertwined the levels we reach can only be
described by a single word

High... I get off her
High... Is the overwhelming feeling that arrives every

      time I ingest her and the flavor frolics on my
      taste buds

My escape route from reality that I don't allow to alter
      my functionality, even though she is my back
      door that leads straight to the backwoods

My stop stressing for free card,
      we converse over any & everything
      laughing & giggling until she's gone & I'm sleep

But when things get too heavy she always comes
      back to lighten my load, tending to my issues
      giving me her sweet release

Maybe the day will come when I no longer wish
      to indulge in her kiss, but until that day
      she'll continue to be my mistress

Her Style

A caramel surprise possibly?
A delectable delight maybe?
Sweet as pure sugar cane with skin smooth
    as freshly carved ivory

A cane is needed as the mere mention of her name
    is crippling to those who verbalize her
    un majestic nature

Marble is used to create idolized moments in time
    where she is marveled at through
    deceiving hypnosis

Majesty describes her perfectly as her presence is
    endowed with what seems like regality, even
    her eyes sparkle like flawless diamonds
Hypnosis is how she eternally enchants her servants
    or should I say lovers whose only purpose is to
    satiate her ferocious craving for life to no avail

Lilacs that are freshly cut is her scent of choice as
    they adorn her bosom accenting her cleaver

exposure

An insatiable appetite is what drives her to their end,
    an appetite for destruction is a more accurate
    description because destruction is described
    as the action of causing so much damage to
    something that it no longer exist
    and destroying is what she is out to do

Mentally stimulating
Visually tantalizing
Physically satisfying
    the motif of thee perfect woman
Maybe too perfect
    maybe not perfect at all,
    not even human maybe?
A siren, a valkyrie, an angel caught in the clutches of
    gravity, maybe something worst, a dark minion,
    a demon, the ultimate seductress, maybe even
    the devil herself
As the old folks say "everything that glitters ain't gold."
So beware of her grasp as she retains the ability to
    Accurately Indiscreetly Destroy Souls

Her Other Man
(Prelude to "The Art Of Hating Myself)

She convinced me that she loved me when she really
    could've cared less I was just a character from
    her dream life that she could actually manifest
I never fathomed her being a cheating bitch like all the
    rest

I had the looks & the taste with the personality to
    match and after a few conversations she called
    me the perfect catch
I wined her and dined her, trying to give her
    everything in my world, and even though it was
    only a few months she knew that to me
    she was more than just my girl
She was my woman, my queen, the one I could focus
    on treating like royalty, because she already
    had my loyalty and I was simply flattered
    out of all the men around she choose me

I gave her my trust but she stole my heart with no
    intention on being my wife see she was an
    actor from the start and got damn shawty

      played that part
And the academy award goes to…..
the grimey bitch who broke my heart

She was a masterpiece walking and easily drew me in
      and she had a voice that could get me to
      commit any sin it always seemed like she was
      speaking to my soul let alone my body
      and she would say just the right things to stir
      up some shit and have me fiending silently
She always made me think of that cliche because with
      her I always felt like I was winning so if loving
      her was wrong I'd just continue on with my
      sinning
The nonsense started with a blocked text or two, but I
      shrugged them off as a wrong number, even
      though my instincts told me different I
      dismissed it because she was the perfect meal
      to satiate my hunger and I thought I needed
      her
I began getting threatening calls & didn't know who to
      blame, had me thinking of my past dealings
      until one day he slipped and said her name

And to be honest, he sounded hurt
    shit I was too, but he was her husband
    so what the fuck was a nigga supposed to do?

My heart was broken yet it still beats
    and I refused to succumb to that feeling of
    defeat
My mind was foggy, yet I could think
    and I refused to act a fool although I was on
    the brink
My vision was blurry, yet I could see
    and that was the moment I refused to ever let
    another woman get the best of me
I contacted her husband saying "ay dude my bad, and
    I mean no disrespect, but your wife you need
    to check cause she's giving up that pussy
    and depositing checks."
"Now I know this is a mess, but you need to know that
    with me there is no stress I'm just gonna chuck
    up the deuces and wish you both the best."

My heart was ripped from my chest so I laid it to rest
    and on the headstone it reads "Here lies a part
    of me I once considered the best."

So now I'm a savage beast in these streets to say the
      very least and every woman I meet looks like
      slab of meat, so I birdman my hands, lick my
      lips and prepare for a feast
Nowadays "How To Be A Player" is my holy grail
      and my actions are fueled by relationships that
      have failed when all I wanted was for her to
      wear white as I lift the veil
      of my wife, but I was her other man so maybe
      in another life
Hopefully I'll see her next lifetime

Complexion 3

Pure Titan

"Regardless of how clean cut or well spoken and handsome they think I'll kidnap their wives and hold them for ransom, give them the Mandingo and prove the fact that once you go black you'll never go back!."

Welcome Back

The movements I have made will forever reverberate
    through the sands of time as generations of the
    future will speak of such in awe
Most of the questions have been answered and
    the inevitable has been conquered
The wholesomeness that was, now only exist in the
    dreams of my past life while what was merely
    temptation is now fully prevalent and running
    ramped as I indulge; tightrope walking across
    the invisible line that divides Heaven & Hell
There is no longer a battle within the confines of my
    mental, but the calm waters of common sense
    have since been evaporated
Leaving behind a dry desolate bed of complexities
    that no longer have an alpha or omega,
        but dwell in the place where bitter memories are
        exiled to exist to be forever forgotten while
        regrets though there's few still remain,
        simply because I've learned to live with them
Thus the rage is amplified...
I understand the task of understanding women
    despite their illogical deference of the ego-trip

      they are constantly on
My reasoning and interpretation goes far beyond the
      ultimately inevitable comprehension of the
      ignorant public as they watch the film that is my
      life with a prejudge mental
Unbeknownst to them I have freed Atlas from his
      curse and added his burden to mine…
La familia, I've been inducted and instructed to treat
      this world as my personal utopia, doing, getting,
      and taking what I want

The relevancy of your life as in comparison to
      mines is highly inadequate
A higher being I am & Mt. Olympus I should be,
      sitting amongst the Gods where mortals
      bow at my feet and shutter at the revelation of
      my voice
I no longer consider my advantage unfair as I now
      realize it is merely God given ability…
Out Think
Out Talk
Out Maneuver
That is the motto as I critically think about
      philosophers and their uncanny likeness to me

as they strategize how to stay three steps ahead
of men & women alike
No Need for formal introductions we've known each
   other our entire lives with the exception of the
   masses who have been reintroduced for
   the first time to thee entity known as
   Eric "Pure Titan" McCain
Hello…and welcome back to my new world order

Dear Poetry

Dear poetry I know you gonna miss me,
    we been together like metaphors & hyperboles,
    syntax with those commas peeking, say a
    couple of words but those letters are secret
Give me a couple of years and I might just sneak in
    a series or two and write circles around you
I will be an author and it'll feel so good, have the
    whole hood saying, "how is he still so good?"
Well I write like floetry poetry, I ain't none of these
    half ass newcomers you know I write notably
I write that heat as the sun comes up, and blast poets
    away like I picked a verbal gun up
Poets back up, they know I ain't no fronta, but how I
    write these words they all think I am a stunna
In all I do I'm trying to advance my quotes
    at any time you'll be the butt of my jokes
But let's not stray from what I came to say to my
    belovedI think we may end ties today, but I really
    love it, so I let it out its cage & hope it comes
    back so I know it's here to stay
It's ripping out my heart, but this time apart is needed
    from the masses who should've gave me stages

Instead they turn they back on this, but my words will
    live on after my casket dip
I'll still enlighten all of my peers, I know they weird ,
    some fear, but I still want them to hear all the
    things that I have to say & they don't have to pay
    I'll still love them though they shun me today
They just like that drunk chick in the club
    you know she a smut, but that mean strut
    make you still wanna fuck
It's like when poets make subliminal poems
    if they ain't directed directly at me they should've
    grabbed they scrotum
You don't really want it with Pure Titan for the record
    I'll expose all your facts for fiction don't be next
    kid
Keep entering that danger zone you gon' make
    Pure Titan put your name in a poem
If you that thirsty for fame muthafucka come on,
    if you just think you might you mine as well
    take ten paces then write
But on another note bout to drop another book
    while I take another tote got damn Pure Titan
    tryna write his way out the hood
I don't pray that I stay out for good even though

anyday a muthafucka could try to play like he
Nas, then I gotta play like Jay-Z, you pass me
the Jay and I'll blaze it away
You poets can't fuck with me, I feel like that dude
the world renowned Langston Hughes
And I ain't tryna fuck my thang up, but I will lay down
a couple couplets and get your throat slit
Now I'm a Desparado, a tough act to follow,
my words will make you lose your head…
Sleepy Hollow
Listen here Poetry baby, I just feel like it's the right
thing to do, I got this brand new chick Literary
Arts and she showing me a lot of action right
now
I know you introduced me to writing and all, but it's
time for me to grow, you gotta let me go baby,
you gotta let me go
I think I'm done for now maybe one for now,
but never gone forever we had fun together
So temporarily we must come to an end,
please show the same love to my friends,
dear poetry

Master of The universe

This is something I had to do for myself to remind
    myself just how fucking powerful I really am

Am I the wittiest?
Am I the prettiest?
Am I the baddest most creative muthatfucka
    low down around this town!?!

I just had to step outside myself to watch myself to get
    an accurate depiction of what a Shogun actually
    looks like... let me proceed

I laid dormant inside of my mother for millennia,
    before I was ever sprinkled like fertilizer
        inside of her fertileness and combined with her
        egg through immaculate conception
I laid cradled in the cradle of her civilization
    creating rivers and mountains through darkness
    and using stars that gave off no light
    as my play things
Becoming bored I became Moses spreading womb
    like Red Sea and all I could see is what I wanted

to be, so as I emerged I spoke one word… free

But I wasn't actually free, you see her essence
    was a part of me and though I could no longer
    hear the music we once created
    I could still feel her tone steady as metronome
    & often times I danced to the rhythm of her
    heartbeat

I came forth through her triangular position of power
    as a deity prepared to rule over humanity,
    because as a king in her womb I already
    conquered the world with a mind
    combined with the intellect of Imhotep
    and the strategic genius of Hannibal Barca
Through metaphors, metamorphosis, and
    metaphysics I am omnipresent, despite time
    I've alway existed
I created railways throughout the solar systems
    so my train of thought could travel through the
    galaxies, I am omnipresent
I am the fire the rained down on Sodom & Gomorrah
    by God's Wrath, I am omnipotent I've been bred
    for this path

So watch me as I grant vision to eyes of hurricanes,
cause hummingbirds to fly in slow motion,
caterpillars to move at speed of light and I
eclipse the night with endless light, please
understand that miracles occur every time
that I write

I've been crumbling conquerors and questioning
what's next

I am that seed that was conceived once
Hera & Hades had sex

It has never been an option to be secondary and all
the police brutality is just a concoction to make
us forget that we are legendary

Yes we reside in a realm where there is a such thing
as a hearse and they are filled with so many
black bodies it's like the whole race is cursed,
but death is never contemplated
when your the master of your universe

So I impregnated the sisters of fate with seeds
of my designed order so they would understand
that my destiny is as bright as the sun's light,
but if I write the word darkness the sun's light
won't shine no more

When I convey my scribes to the people
> it's the opposite of evil and more like God's will
> incarnated into words, now that may sound
> absurd, but to make sure you heard allow me
> to break it down for you

When I recite I produce a down of feather from my
> vocal chords that look wing like but when used
> right they sound like the trumpet blowing for
> Armageddon, because after me there is no more

My demons only fight me when I'm dreaming,
> because when I'm awake my presence alone
> causes hell to quake and I understand the
> understood needs not to be said,
> so when I do verbalize it personifies my wrath
> and everything that stands before me is dead

So I ask you… "AM I THE MASTER!"

One Page

It's funny because this has been on my mind lately. Having a fresh pencil, a crisp piece of loose sleeve & that one page ain't enough. How the fuck am I suppose to fit all these tight ass lines on one page. It's so many different ways to express myself, translating to the people with my words how I play this game called life and one page ain't enough.

It's crazy how things change faster than time flies
    the more that I write dope the more that y'all get high, the more that I write down the more that your chick smile, cause I'm a dope ass poet making her life worthwhile
Langston Hughes status, E. Badu on the dash and
    I'm smooth as Barack Obama cruising in a Cadillac... Seville, feel me words on the real I'm one of the last poets so listen so you can hear

Writing like Vita Colon these words she must
    condone, all I see is my future and I'm writing it all alone

All I wanted was to write, but one page ain't enough
    cause I be filling notebooks, about 15 every
    month

I'm far from being rich, but, not exactly poor
    and everything that I write was never written
    before
Putting on at these functions to keep your minds from
    lunching, while I'm dressed fresher than your
    pastor, but smelling like marijuana

I'm tryna get me a chick fine like the Honey Bee,
    Bria McCormick status with that black girl magic
Rocking all this Steve Madden your old lady love my
    fashion and I'm writing all this heat, peep how
    my paper is stacking

You better put away some poems for the rainy days,
    so your words live forever fuck fading away
Writing like James Baldwin these lines just fall in,
    I started off with a notion now I'm flowing like an
    ocean

They say my words ice, don't get froze for the night,
> my brother Xay died after graduation damn what
> a memory

Tryna get to the top of hill after starting from the ave,
> tryna follow my dreams so all my kids can have

Now I get paid when people hear me,
> reciting all my soul words so sincerely

People hate that I'm out here killing everything
> tryna leave a legacy for my young kings

Savagery

It always showed up in a monsoon of horrendously
    spoken words coming from the most handsome
    mouth you've ever encountered
    creating sentences that sounded just as good as
    I looked
You were drawn to me & the harder you fought to
    resist the faster you would end up back in my
    clutches, tangled in my web yearning for comfort
    amidst my sheets and though none came,
    you always would
Recalling the bad times of when I would sing a lullaby
    to you telling you how you needed me
    & being with you wasn't an option,
    because I'd be gone when the wind blew
Even though you realized I didn't love you too
    your feelings you managed after coming an
    to an understanding that I was a savage
You became a fiend for the hurt I caused,
    no longer being functional without its crushing
    embrace and although you were already self
    injurious your cutting was no longer enough
    and you needed the pain I caused

I often wonder if it was me you loved or the hurt
    since your heart ached for its presence,
    but the thoughts would never last long
    & I would be focused on another woman
    singing another lullaby
I guess that's the advantage of being a savage

Sister

A wise man once said,
    "the difference between good and great is that
    good wasn't built to last."
Sweetheart you are reversely the last of the greats,
    a mythical creature like that of a goddess who
    holds a seat on the council of higher beings that
    reigns supreme atop the mighty Mt. Olympus
    with the strength of an ever devoted dragon and
    the uncanny beauty of a unicorn

Through long days & longer nights together
    we have weathered the storm
Amidst thunderous arguments
    lightning fast accusations and
    a downpour of suspicion
Where were you?
Who was she?
Did you kiss her?
Indeed I did and the woman in your questioning
    is that of your sister

Being great in reverse leaves you plain and simply
>just being good

You see I shamelessly worship your sisters dichotomy
>and she is solely and holistically thee,
>>last of the greats

The closer she gets to amazing from great
>the further you go from good to nothing

She holds a seat on the council
>of the most high

She carries me over my troubles & doubts
>with her dragon like strength

She calms my seas of disparity
>wit her unicorn like beauty

Through long days of bliss & longer nights of lust
>we have weathered your storm

Your thunder, lightning, nor rain
>can hinder our happiness

Heartless
>maybe

A monster
> maybe that too

But it's your sister who I'll be with,
> because I'm not in love with you

In My Bag

Some say my actions are those of cockiness
    I tell them there of confidence because
    cockiness would be me taking your girl out
    & she spending your dead presidents
There are a few out here I noticed that's counterfeit,
    I'm speaking in reference to these lames
    who are illiterate
Can't read the signs nor can they write
    their own game plan
Thinking their by my side leaving footprints
    in the sand when in actuality they're in my
    shadow because they are not their own man
Are these poetic bars?
Never, I keep those in the locker, I'm just here to
    shout out the blockers and Pure Titan jockers
Anyway back on track
    I'll scoop your sister in the black on black
    and it's a cavalier at that... HA!
I know what your thinking
    I'm on my shit & reading this poem is a sign,
    but on the contrary your on your shit in reverse
    so technically that's puts you on mine

My SWAG is on an impeccable level,
    it's blasphemy speaking against me like
    talking slick to oil or talking black to a kettle
Some say I'ma poetical lyricist,
    and I be writing scribes hotter than
    the son of the morning, I have their son's
    mourning in the morning, cause their
    fathers not heavenly and his heads not
    adorning a crown of thorns instead his head
    was riddled with metaphorically written
    wit-tipped bullets that will belittle any little
    minded person who is willing to trace me,
    but there is only 1 Dictionary, 1 Paparazzi,
    1 WordSmith
If I had to put a title to these words
    I'd call it Poetical Wrath Riff

Complexion 4

Syne

"I'll beat the pussy up like we're having a fight, just call me Ike and I'll kiss it afterwards to make me feel alright… I remain chivalrous."

Positions

Chester French said it best, we'll be cool as long as
    you just play your part, but this convo is baffling
    because you knew what this was from the start
    no commitment, no feelings just good times
    when we dealing no questions or cues cause
    you know what we do

Relish in each other's presence & savor one anothers
    essence, eating our desires & drinking our lust,
    we may not smoke, but we definitely gonna
    fuck

The intricacies of our lives have nothing to do with
    one another as long as we doin it and doin it
    and doin it well we'll keep policies like the army
    don't ask & don't tell

There are rules of engagement, a code of conduct to
    follow and any deviation from the plan puts in
    jeopardy our tomorrow, because there's
    nothing set in stone except we always go home
    no stay overs or layovers go down after we
    bone and no calls or text after 7 when it comes
    to the phone

Now don't get it twisted the attraction is more than
    just physical, cause in order to get this "D"
    you gotta stimulate my mental and not with
    pillow talk or exchanging secrets, but
    intellectual conversation so we know who were
    sleeping with
We can speak on politics, religion, the arts, & sports
    with an undertone of sex so the basis
    of our situation we're unable to distort
You stay in your lane & I'll stay in mine & when our
    paths cross neither of us will mind
There's no straddling the fence over how or where
    we'll begin, our eyes lock intensely and we
    go right in... licking & kissing & touching
    & fucking and as far as limits go
    we speak on nothing
Its' no holds barred when we're intertwined,
    but in case one gets tested a safe word is
    defined
50 Shades of Syne she love this playroom of mines
    and we work well together because we keep
    open minds

Life's transitions keep us constantly missing,
> but we can stay on one accord as long as we stick to the mission & when there's speech to be heard we both shut up n listen

This can last for a while or until we grow apart
> just remember we can be cool as long as you just play your part

Doused

There were no signs posted on your shore,
    just a seemingly endless ocean
    no lifeguards watching to warn me that this
    would be no ordinary swim
No way of knowing that my flames could be doused
    before I ever got in
10,000 leagues under the sea, yet to handle this
    my ancestors would have to be from Atlantis
    even though Jacques Cousteau has always
    been an idol of mine
Poppa warned me not to jump in the deep end
    if I couldn't swim, but I've become an aquaphile
    when it comes to you
Keep soaking me, giving me oxygen to breathe
    as you continuously submerge me in
    liquified excerpts of sensual gratification that
    pours out of you waterboarding me
    and as a sadist I could get use to this
I just wanna keep drowning amidst your sweet water
    rapids pushing your pleasure palate to
    maximum exposure, I keep you lit,
    you keep me drenched

Fire and water are opposites but make a perfect fit

Tatted

Her skin... so radiant, brown, unblemished or scarred
    by life's interesting ways of reminding us
    of what once was

Whether draped in linen or in her most glorious
    exposed state her skin, that milk chocolate skin
    taunts me, teasing me, beckoning and pleading
    with me to come to its aide
    and rescue it from the monotony of its
    mundane existence
To replace a space that was normally visible
    chocolatey goodness with something that will
    tell a story of our encounter...
A tattoo which is something new to her and her
    skin,that brown skin that requires me to be so
    close that there's no telling where mines end
    and hers begin.
"Are you sure this is what you want?"
    I asked with a smile so sinister the devil herself
    would think twice if she wanted to embark on
    this journey

She simply nodded her head and although no words
 were said her silence was thick with sultry
 seduction and a yearning desire
 and as I sat back to admire my blank chocolate
 canvas my brain caught fire tryna decide where
 I would start, what I would do, how deep I
 would go, when would be the best time to
 strike and why... why has this perfect slate of
 chocolate marble not been chiseled and
 transformed into someone's variation of beauty
 with everlasting marks that would render calm
 to my perturbed mind as I give and pleasurable
 pain as she receives

Kissing her isn't all I could think of nor was it all I
 wanted to do, but it served as an aphrodisiacal
 prelude of what's to come
Lip kisses, ear nibbles, neck sucks, and shoulder
 hhhmmm, those beautifully bare soft chocolate
 shoulders that cause my vampiric instincts to
 take over
I sank my teeth in aggressively timid to begin the
 session and the initial sensation is so euphoric
 I get an erection, aroused by the power I feel

She moaned from pleasure and writhed in pain
>fearfully curious about how far submitting to my lustful desires will take her

I took a journey from the top of her head to the soles of her feet exploring her body conquering it in parts, tattooing each one creating reminders of these moments and a blueprint of how to appease her new fetish

Within our encounters there are teeth marks and moans which are actually the tattoos on her skin that are shown and the sound of ecstasy as her mind is blown
As her late night lover we enjoy many things like being tied up and subdued,
but during the day even though I can't stay she'll still have her tattoos
She can never forget me

A Mile Up

Take off is lovely & I have a smooth window seat
    overlooking the cities wondering who I am going
    to meet
A bad bitch or a cold freak actually either will do
    cause I'm long overdue

I left my girl at home, so on this plane it is just us,
    guaranteed if she finds out it'll be more than a
    fuss and something closer to a fight
So no cellphones, no emails, no forms of
    communication we will sit accompanied by
    admiration and the sounds of the plane
    mixed with these nasty freaky thoughts
    that's all on my brain

Limited speech, lite conversing, mainly just
    body language & flirting
She chewed something with a familiar hue
    & the scent of nostalgia,she used a few words
    to talk to me, but her eyes spoke louder
They screamed at me, and all I heard was mile high
    inductee, I was hype on the inside

    but my cool outward demeanor said "feel free"
She said, "allow me to translate your movements not
    into words, but actions as your every molecule is
    preparing for what is about to happen

I told myself If I could I would
Vanilla love on a plane, sky high, while sky high
    and getting higher off the moment because
    I know that I own it at least for the moment
    and that silky soft throat, please allow me
    another toke
She said, "all puffing no passing this a personal party
    and although we know each other hardly rest
    assure in the fact that we are in the air over
    somewhere and for this red eye flight I did
    prepare to take you where you need to be and I
    mean these words wholeheartedly."
"We have the same destination a place of great
    elation and overwhelming sensation similar to a
    vacation, but to be a member of the mile high
    nation you must make a donation,
    I mean it's just a little motivation for this oral
    examination."
You know I obliged

Now a member of a prestigious club I exit the plane
    still feeling like I'm above the clouds and I'm
    proud speed walking to the car to spark up the
    loud and send out a tweet saying,
    "just call me Ace Mcloud"
After that I made a vow that while on a plane
    to speak not with my mouth,
    but only with my eyes, because the understood
    needs not to be said when your flying a mile high

Chocolate Eclipse

I have a certain lust for life and if everything goes as it
    should I'll be tasting you tonight
The moon is shining bright but I don't want that in my
    sight so bring that ass here girl & let me tell you
    about my blithe
I have a craving for you so come step into my view
    and sit that chocolate pussy on my face
    to feed this craving with a taste
We had a great time on our date and I understand it's
    getting late, but I must inquire about your flavor
    so baby let me just taste you and we can fuck
    later
I'm all for infiltration, but if I give you this penetration
    we'll both be yawning because you & I know
    how swiftly work comes in the morning
So we'll hold off on the my body all over your body
    although the way that dress is hugging them
    thighs I can tell you do pilates, got me feeling
    like Usher singing whoa Kimosabi
But I'll still feel your amazing grace, but instead of
    wrapping your legs around my waist you'll be
    straddling my face, but baby we can play it safe

I won't even scrape the plate,
I'll eat just enough so that nut you bust
our lust it can satiate
Now the time for talking is over so throw them legs
over my shoulders and let me kiss those lower
lips, I promise you'll love being
my chocolate eclipse

Written All Over

Woman, I will write all over you…

My pen will send all of your freaky little secrets to the
    light and bring the most sexual fantasies your
    mind can imagine to life
I wanna create the desires of your pussy with the tip
    my pen and before the ink dries we'll be at it
    again

Woman, I will write all over you...

I'd like to treat you like a book with no words
    & open you wide as I scribble my scribes inside
    and write deep into your pages
    as I describe a story that is new & bold
    yet still comes off as ageless
A story of passion, a story of desire, a story so
    intimate & erotic that reading the words will
    set your soul on fire

Woman, I will write all over you...

As I turn your pages and explore your content
        examining your body and lifting the veil
listening to the pulse of your pussy to see
        what it will tell as if I'm Hellen Keller
        deciphering braille
Oh what a feeling when I dive in your embrace
        there are nights I want nothing more than to fall
        back and allow you to just sit on my face
        in hopes your most complex content will seep
        into my skin

Woman, I will write all over you…

Black Kisses

You know that feeling you can't describe
      and all you can give are fanciful theatrics
      of what words can't accurately depict
Like when she kisses me everything is sucked outta
      me like I'm Will Ferrel in that one movie,
      you know the one when the leech is attached
      to his back, and never mind
I believe it's called land of the lost
Anyway, everything about her is soft from her feet
      up to her thighs and eyes and I love feeling the
      curves of her hips as she caresses me with
      the curves of her lips and speaking of lips,
      that MAC black lipstick
When she kisses me with it I go into a fit of rage
      like Lu Kang in Mortal Kombat when they killed
      Johnny Cage and even though I want to be the
      hero it feels so good I'm frozen like Sub-Zero
      and all I wanna do is melt in her mouth
Black kisses

They can only be compared to, well they are really
      incomparable, but if I actually had to this is

what I'd do, I'd say they're like teasing images
of heavenly black beauty like Serena Williams
ascending to the clouds and having a perfect
view of her booty, which would render calm to
the most perturbed of minds and I want this
forever so please don't mind but I need you to
be mine

Black Kisses

I just want her to bear hug me with her lips
    & smear that MAC black lipstick
    all over this dick
I love the way she kiss on me because she
    simultaneously licks on me and when
    it's time for her to go I never want her to leave,
    if I could I would chain her to the bed like that
    chick from misery minus the drugged tea
    and sledge hammer of course
I just want her lips to marry my dick without possibility
    of divorce so I can keep those black kisses all
    to myself without an ounce of remorse,
    gggoooottttt DAMN

Black Kisses

Mental Inbox

I noticed you noticing me while I was noticing you in the club and I wanted to put you on notice that I noticed you, but I was too shy. So I just put myself on notice about the recent notification and thus began my fantasy

This twisted mentality of mine that eats through
    my logic and devours my rationale
    is reacting with the fire that blazes deep in my
    loins sending me into a hypnotic daze every
    time I see you

Am I becoming drunk by thinking about your touch
    or is this angel in my view slyly intoxicating me
    though mental tequila filled kisses

Kissing… sipping… kissing… sipping

Now in a drunken stupor hunger engulfs my senses
    and tasting your love stains the looking glass of
    my thought process rendering my mind useless

Causing me to only be able to see just how perfectly
    your hips fit over my shoulders,
        to hear your moans of pleasure and my slurps
        of delight, to smell the wondrous aroma of your
        love, and to taste your flavor that I will indeed
        savor and make you my fav-or-
It is no denying that when Syne shows up your
    guaranteed to fall in love with words like me
    licking similes off of your titties or giving a
    metaphoric kiss to your clit

Thinking to myself is your love the flavor of ambrosia,
    the food of the Gods
Aphrodite herself partook of such a delectable delight,
    but I doubt she ever tasted anything quite like
    you

I licked my lips and ruffled my goatee as this day
    wonder was taking control of me
Visualizing my lips on your lips & my tongue on your
    clit, giving a sensual seduction leading to a
    sexual eruption

Under your hypnosis I have no control of my actions
        as if your love is enchanted
So possibly I'm punch drunk, or it may be likely that
        I'm love drunk, but I'm pretty sure I'm probably
        pussy drunk so fuck a threesome a foursome is
        what I want, my mouth your pussy, your mouth
        my dick

My twisted mentality and my mouth yearns, craves,
        and needs your flavor so if drunk I am than
        baby drunk I will be
You see we stand together across the club,
        mentally stripped wearing nothing but each
        others eyes
Nipples hard, pussy wet… muscles tight, dick rock,
        but alas

I merely noticed you noticing me while I was noticing you in the club and I wanted to put you on notice that I noticed you, but I was too shy. So I just put myself on notice about the recent notification and thus began the fantasy

Insatiable

There are moments I may scope a woman
>from across the room, she is nonchalantly
being herself & by no means am I being stealth,
I am blatant and want my intrigue to be known
Never have you ever been tangled amidst the mist of
them knowing your thoughts are those of sin,
hoping you can slip on in and sip on them
like a glass of cognac as they sit on my
shoulders like an animal skin, never
have you ever been
I prefer for it to be hot and sticky as I blaze that ass
like I do my icky, only puffing no passing this is a
personal party
Never have I ever had licked lips expose my affliction
so that I can't help but give in to my addiction,
no longer denying, but embracing all the things
their bodies whisper to me & although history
repeats itself this being I've become is
completely something else as I have created
a lane, a God amongst mortals and sex
is my domain

So having two or more women is just right to see who
    can handle me for a whole night while I beat
    the pussy up like we're having a flight,
    just call me Ike and I'll kiss it afterwards to make
    me feel alright, as I remain chivalrous
Never have you ever made a video to see how far
    she'll go and although she's the feature
    you're the star of the show so facial or swallow
    how far will she go?
See baby we can suck on one another until we're
    tasting each other and what's craved is the
    sensation of me giving penetration,
    women love how my shit be hard just right
Never has he ever told a female she shit out of luck if
    she's tryna sleep because he wants to be tongue
    deep in-between her thighs tryna suck her soul
    through her pussy until it reaches his insides
    like he is Shang Tsung… "Your soul is mine!"
Females thirst for me to be biting on their nipples like
    their nursing me, while I'm so deep in the pussy
    it's like reverse birthing me
Never have I ever had to ask "you almost there yet?"
    cause I'll make a woman cum so many times
    she'll get you, me, her, she, we us, they,

here and there wet & I ain't talking bout sweat
so I'll drink it like fine wine until it ain't nothing left
With soaking lips I'm drowning slowly in this sweet
sticky shit, so my tongue draws outlines on their
skin, giving a tantalizing sensation they don't
want to end so I get one off and we begin again,
because I am insatiable and never have you
ever been

Special Acknowledgements

A Fallen Kings Prince

We place his name upon our lips &
    memories we reminisce while shooting the
    shit
With friends and family who do the same
    confirming that his death was not in vain
    and for ever more in our hearts will our love
    for him reign
As loved ones gather round a few warm
    tears may hit the ground, but smiles from
    thoughts of him on our faces are found
We remember Za for more than
    his last quest and put bread in the jukebox
    upon request and corporate thug as shots of
    Remy and Henny burn our chest
Amidst our sorrow & celebration there is one
    that deserves our concentration
King Za we all mourn as the fallen one, but
    who must be raised is Za the prince his
    only son

He may have a heavy heart & a shining
        crown but it's our job to keep him lifted up
        so he never feels down and vow to him
        every year and every day we never let his
        father's memory fade away

He'll grow strong & stand tall as a man
        facing the world's bumps & stings while
        bringing honor to his father a fallen king

RIP ZA

A Mothers Love

When I think of my mother the question of "how?
"comes to mind, how did you have the energy
to deal with me and that brother of mine,
not to mention be a friend, a chauffeur and a
cook all the while showing us the ways of the
world like an open book
A single mom doing it all, yet still made sure we were
supported and felt loved, you nursed us, taught
us and counseled us and made sure we were
provided for with everything from wisdom to
hugs
I know raising us two you had to have some
assistance from above cause I know it wasn't
easy raising two boys with love

Not taking any nonsense, but always allowing boys to
be boys having had you in my life I can say has
been one of my greatest joys, because a
mothers love is endless and enduring, it is
created from sacrifice and pain, making a
mothers love something that can
not be explained
It is felt, and experienced whether it is deserved or
not, a mothers love is not something that
comes with conditions it is patient and kind
and most definitely forgiving

Your memory like your love will be felt forever,
    and through trials and storms we have
    weathered together

As an angel I know you will continue to guide the kids
    and I as they all grow up one after another,
    so I thank God for your life and the gift
    of being able to call you my mother

RIP MOM GAIL

Published By Books Speak For You Publishing

Specializing In 7 & 21 Day Publishing

Publishing In Over 100 Languages

267-318-8933

Printed In The United States

www.Booksspeakforyou.com

www.ingramcontent.com/pod-product-compliance
Lightning Source LLC
Chambersburg PA
CBHW071008160426
43193CB00012B/1974